RIGHT PERSON-RIGHT JOB
GUESS OR KNOW

The Breakthrough Technologies of Performance Information

by Chuck Russell

Johnson & James, Atlanta

Published by: Johnson & James
                   12460 Crabapple Road
                   Suite 202-113
                   Alpharetta, GA 30201 _

Printed and bound by: Data Reproductions Corporation
                           Rochester Hills, Michigan

Library of Congress Cataloging in Publication Data
Russell, Chuck
   Right Person - Right Job, Guess or Know
(The Breakthrough Technologies of Performance Information).
Library of Congress Catalog Card Number: 95-074751

ISBN 0-9647793-0-7

Dedication

To my parents who believed in me from the beginning

To my wife, Lauretta, who believed in me when it wasn't easy

To Lacey and Jamey who believe I can do anything

To Jim Sirbasku, Dick Hunter, Bob Quigley, and Harold Goldbortin, who taught me to believe in me

Acknowledgements

My special thanks to Donna Johnston and the incredibly talented artists of Finished Art in Atlanta, Georgia for creating the cover art and guiding me far beyond where I saw to go.

My thanks to Denise Holland, Leigh Skole and the Printing Industry Association of Georgia for the use of the cover art, which originally appeared in a cover story in the *Georgia Printer*.

My thanks to Ray Bouléy for his remarkable imagination and encouragement.

My thanks to Jim Silavent for making me sit down and write instead of just talking.

My thanks to Ralph Tanner for his unselfish advice, and for his insistence on quality.

My thanks to my partner, Julie Moreland and my company for their combined patience and support.

My thanks to Bobby Cottrell and Image Avenue for the graphic design and layout of the book that made it both interesting and easy to read.

My thanks to Norvin Hagan at Geographics for generous support and advice.

*Today, the use of
assessment information
is no longer an option.*

*The legal environment
demands it.*

*Maintaining a competitive
advantage requires it.*

The purpose of this book is to help you
make good decisions that expand potential,
not limit it; strengthen your legal compliance,
not increase your exposure; and introduce
you to a technology that is revolutionizing
the way businesses understand people
and their performance.

Table of Contents

Table of Contents

Introduction

When I attended Georgia Tech in 1968, the school pointed with pride to the Univac computer, which occupied a significant amount of floor space in the Computer Sciences Building. Majoring in Industrial Management, I dutifully spent hours keypunching the cards to run, rerun, and rerun my rudimentary programs until the great machine ate them with approval, spewing out reams of computer paper hours later. . . if I was lucky. Twenty-four years later, I am writing this book on a super fast computer with many, many megabytes, high resolution color monitor and a CD-ROM drive.

I am embarrassed to admit that for years I denied the need for such technological marvels, debated a hundred and one reasons why computers were not necessary, were not as personal, and in general, lacked a number of essential intangible qualities that I don't seem to remember just now. The foundation of my unwillingness to embrace progress was simply my lack of understanding of what was really possible and how easy it was to learn the new skills.

Today, the vast majority of business people share a parallel experience when dealing with testing and assessments. Most of their experience with testing is from another era (in many cases even if it was purchased last week). Comparative knowledge about psychometric instruments is generally biased if provided by a test publisher, or complex and esoteric when provided by psychologists. Lacking effective knowledge, some well-meaning attorneys and business consultants have advised clients to avoid such things altogether. While such an extremely conservative approach may have kept our prehistoric ancestors from entering the cave with the sabre-toothed tiger in it, in today's rapidly changing world of business, it yields an important advantage to your competition.

I have written this book, and indeed have structured my company, to enable business people to understand the dramatic and far-reaching changes that the new technology of performance information is having on the world today. Questions that have puzzled managers for generations can be answered. Strategic planning of human resources can be done on a scale never before imagined. Within a decade, bad job fits will be obsolete. The management and training of people will attain a focus that will transform almost every concept and philosophy taught today.

This is not a psychological text, although the psychological concepts are sound. This is not a legal text, although the legal concepts are sound. This is a book written for business people, to help you make better decisions; or ask better questions; or simply think new ideas.

Positively,
Chuck Russell

Chapter 1

THE PROBLEM WITH THE WAY IT'S ALWAYS BEEN DONE

"Businesses spend an enormous amount of time, energy, and money in a never ending effort to train, coach, or motivate marginal employees to a level of merely adequate performance."

4

THE PROBLEM WITH THE WAY IT'S ALWAYS BEEN DONE

Someone once observed that all unhappiness is caused by comparison, and in a very real sense, that sort of comparison is the purpose of this book. But rather than unhappiness, the book seeks to inspire a constructive discontent with some old ideas and some old methodology. It seeks to reveal that extraordinarily exciting and somewhat scary landscape of potential opportunities that result from a true technological breakthrough.

Today engineering students use high tech, multifunction calculators instead of slide rules, ten thousand-item inventories are easily managed with computer information systems that not only track it more accurately and faster, but generally with less expense. Oversized composite tennis racquets have not only made wooden racquets obsolete, but have changed the very strategies of the game. Overnight delivery services, fax machines, and E-mail have altered the character of communications.

As commonplace as these examples may seem now, a few years ago the concepts were unimaginable. Yet in each case, a few thought leaders seized the opportunity to establish a sustainable competitive advantage in their field. It was their constructive discontent with the way it had always been done that inspired their actions.

In every business throughout the world, there are people who are not performing as expected. At some time, virtually every person has been in a job that was not right. Yet every business hired those people with careful thought and positive expectations. Every person took those jobs with the intention of succeeding. The tragedy is that these results are accepted as being normal.

Within a few years, such things will be looked on with the same curious tolerance that is today reserved for wooden tennis racquets and businesses without computers or fax machines. Driven by the quantum leaps in computer technology, psychometrics, the science of measuring the behavior of people, has seen tremendous breakthroughs in recent years. The nature of these breakthroughs will redefine the concepts of how to place the right person in the right job. The scope of these breakthroughs will initiate a rethinking of every people-related aspect of business.

Managing Systems vs.
Managing People

BUSINESSES HAVE TWO KINDS OF PROBLEMS:

SYSTEMS   PEOPLE

- ▲ Objective Information   ▲ Observation
- ▲ Quantified Information   ▲ Opinion
- ▲ Common Frame   ▲ Emotion
  of Reference

**SYSTEMS PROBLEMS ARE EASIER TO SOLVE
BECAUSE BETTER INFORMATION IS AVAILABLE.**

Historically, businesses have been much more successful at solving systems problems. With systems problems, there is the benefit of dealing with:

- objective information
- quantified information
- a common frame of reference

With people problems, managers generally base their actions on much less reliable sources such as:

- observation
- opinion
- emotion

Observation is problematical because the frenzied, long hours of the disorganized worker can appear more dedicated than the relaxed, even casual approach of some top performers.

Advice based on **opinion** is valid only to the degree that the circumstances and people involved are the same as the ones of past experience.

Human beings ride the waves of **emotion**. Unfortunately, businesses too often conclude that if revenues are up, the employees are doing it right; and if revenues drop, the employees are doing it wrong.

> *"Systems problems are simply easier to solve because better information is available."*

Despite the inherent weakness of these sources of information, businesses pursue solutions to people problems with no less intensity than solutions for systems problems. **Systems problems are simply easier to solve because better information is available.**

8

Russell's Rule of Thirds

In any population of people, whether it is composed of managers, salespeople, mechanics, or hockey players, one third are top performers; one third are OK performers; and one third are questionable performers.

Businesses tend to celebrate the "Terrific" performers, lament the "Questionable" performers, and ignore the "OK" performers. In reality, effective businesses, having good systems and good products, make money with "OK" performers; "Terrific" performers are just icing on the cake. The real disaster for profitability is with "Questionable" performers. Businesses spend an enormous amount of time, energy, and money in a neverending effort to train, coach, or motivate the "Questionable" to a level of merely adequate performance. This is like training members of a swimming team on how not to drown. It may save their lives, but it certainly won't win the team any medals.

This presents a remarkable opportunity for any business to catapult itself to a higher level of success. If that same time, energy, and money can be focused on the "OK" and the "Terrific" groups, tremendous benefits can be achieved.

Businesses Have Three Opportunities to Impact the Performance of their People

The First of these is at the Front Door

The Selection Process is clearly the most important point of action in terms of impacting the productivity and profitability of a business. In a competitive market, each company must strive to improve the level of talent in its pool of employees. Each new hire has the potential to enhance the overall performance to the company, or to diminish that performance. Too often the selection process has become a seldom successful search for the next "Superstar" of

11

that industry. In reality, well-run businesses make money with average-performance employees... if they can avoid hiring too many below average-performance employees. In baseball, it is not the lack of grandslam homeruns or no-hit games that keep a team out of the World Series. The difference is generally in the games that could have been won except for the dropped fly ball, the hanging curve ball, the ill-timed steal, or some other fundamental error. When those kinds of errors can be avoided, the "superstar plays" just seem to happen on their own. If businesses can avoid hiring "Questionable performers", every now and then a "Superstar" just seems to appear.

> *"well-run businesses make money with average-performance employees.... if they can avoid hiring too many below average-performance employees"*

The second reason why the selection process is vital to profitability is that it is the most economical point to exit marginal performers from the company. Initial expenses accumulate rapidly: post-offer medical exams, benefits enrollment, unemployment insurance, personnel staffing time, training programs, orientation time, interaction with existing employees, interaction with management and supervisors, and so on. There are other intangibles that accumulate once the "questionable performer" is hired: the effect on company standards, the effect on employee attitudes, the effect on client or customer perceptions, the effect on supervisory attitudes, and of course, many others. These effects and expenses comprise the much-debated cost of turnover. It is much-debated because estimates range from mere thousands of dollars to many times an employee's annual salary. Some companies actually cultivate a

12

certain level of turnover as a means of renewing their organization. Others have even asserted that since their personnel departments and human resource departments were on salary, there was effectively no cost for turnover. While such statements are naive at best, they serve to underscore the frustration and lack of manageability that many companies have been conditioned to accept as a part of the hiring process. **The most thorough selection process imaginable costs less than hiring the wrong person for even a day in most companies.**

> *" The most thorough selection process imaginable costs less than hiring the wrong person for even a day in most companies."*

Changes in the legal environment have served to further emphasize the critical importance of designing an effective selection process. Important, and in many cases, long-overdue legislation has been enacted providing equal opportunities for employment to all people. Laws such as the Americans with Disabilities Act and the numerous Civil Rights Acts prohibit any form of **unfairly discriminatory** hiring practices. The difficulty for businesses is that selection processes are always fundamentally discriminatory…they serve to discriminate which candidates are most likely to succeed at a particular job. Selecting the best candidate for the job is exactly what is intended by the business and the legislation.

The problem occurs when businesses lack an objective measure of job suitability. Three unfortunate choices are often the result. In one case, fearful of being accused of unfair discrimination, the business unwittingly hires unqualified minorities. Their subse-

13

quent marginal performance reinforces the belief that minorities cannot do the job. In the second case, the business avoids the unfamiliar by not hiring any minorities. This costs the business good employees and sets up a potential legal problem. In the third case, the business becomes ultra-conservative. Now fearful of either extreme, the business plays it safe by minimizing any change or turnover. It attempts to fill all jobs internally or from within a very narrow network of known candidates. This seriously restricts the company's growth and development.

Today it is not necessary to accept the risk of marginal performance that is inherent in traditional hiring methods. It is possible to effectively and economically select the right person for the right job, objectively, with no unfair discrimination. This freedom from uncertainty enables a business to pursue a course of positive and dynamic growth.

> *"Today it is not necessary to accept the risk of marginal performance that is inherent in traditional hiring methods."*

The Second is After They are Hired

Unfortunately once a marginal employee has been hired, it takes time before the problem becomes apparent ... and time is expensive. At best, it generally takes about a month before the new employee's performance is recognized as marginal. This is because of the inevitable "honeymoon period", when the new employee is concentrating on creating the best impression, and coincidently, the supervisor is most forgiving. This is the time of that most deviously expensive concept ... the learning curve. It is devious because too often no one seems to know exactly how long the learning curve should be. It is expensive because every day that the new employee cannot perform at an experienced level involves

15

costs in terms of opportunities missed, resources invested in that employee, and the effect on the other members of the work team who must compensate during the training period.

Once the shortcomings are identified, most supervisors will spend at least another month attempting to coach or train the new employee to an adequate level of performance. If the supervisor is forced to spend time with marginal employees, then that time is not available for the successful performers. The irony is that good performers generally benefit the most from effective coaching.

Sometimes incentive programs are created in an attempt to encourage a higher level of performance or alter the behavior of marginal employees. These programs generally are more effective with the better performers.

16

The Last is at the Back Door

If these methods prove to be unsuccessful, the business is left with the most expensive alternative. That is to either redeploy the marginal employee to another department and hope for better results, or to exit the employee from the company. Unfortunately all of the time, energy, and money invested in the employee leaves with them. Now the process must begin all over.

17

Chapter 2

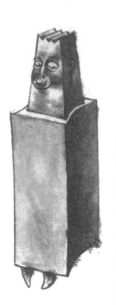

A NEW PARADIGM FOR UNDERSTANDING PEOPLE AND THEIR PERFORMANCE

"It is difficult and expensive to train your way out of a bad hiring decision."

A NEW PARADIGM FOR UNDERSTANDING PEOPLE AND THEIR PERFORMANCE

The Selection Process is clearly the most critical and controllable variable in the development of a productive work team. Yet here, traditional methodology has several inherent limitations in terms of understanding people and their performance.

Classically businesses have viewed people and performance within the context of ability. Those with a lot of ability could do almost anything well, and those with lesser ability were more limited. This paradigm supports the belief that education, training, and experience will serve to enhance ability and therefore, performance. If people with the ability did not perform well after being trained, the problem was assumed to be motivational.

Actually, this ability potential rests upon a three-part foundation of Attitude (Company Fit), Technical Competencies (Skills Match), and the concept of Job Fit, which has only recently been easily and accurately measurable. Job Fit refers to how well an individual's cognitive abilities, interests, and personality traits match those required for success in a particular job. It is this critical relationship between the job and the person's Job Fit that shatters the myth of the traditional ability concept. If a person fits the job, training and experience can definitely enhance performance (ability). If a person does not fit the job, neither training, experience, or any other program is likely to seriously improve performance (ability).

19

THE CORNERSTONES OF JOB PERFORMANCE

An effective Selection Process consists of three distinct parts:
- Company Fit (attitude, grooming, mannerisms, ethics, etc.)
- Skills Match (experience, abilities, certification, etc.)
- Job Fit (cognitive abilities, personality structure, interests)

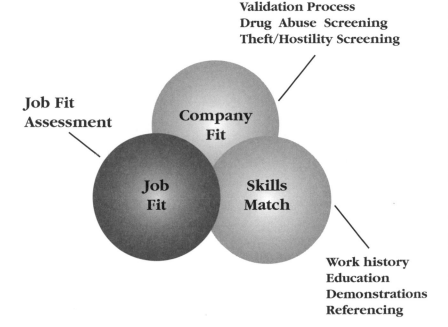

Interview Process
Validation Process
Drug Abuse Screening
Theft/Hostility Screening

Job Fit Assessment

Company Fit

Job Fit

Skills Match

Work history
Education
Demonstrations
Referencing

The Ideal Candidate Will Match In Each Part

20

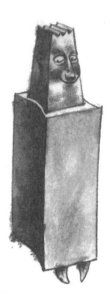

Company Fit is the degree to which the candidate's attitudes, values, ethics, and grooming fit those required by the position. Face-to-face interviews are typically used to evaluate these things. Factors such as honesty, being drug-free, and not being prone to hostility are other important elements. These can be determined using various paper and pencil tests, electronic tests, chemical tests, and background checks.

There is no substitute for face-to-face interviewing. The perceptions, intuitions, and experience-based observations of a well-trained interviewer are invaluable in assessing certain qualities of attitude and fit with a company's culture. There are intrinsic problems however, that are inescapable, even to professional interviewers.

The Halo Effect occurs when interviewers see a part of themselves in the candidates. It may be a common experience, a common school, a common sport, or some other shared background. It may be a similar characteristic of personality that generates a positive feeling of recognition. Whatever it may be, this "self-recognition" generates a halo that can cause a relatively mediocre resumé to glow with merit. **Unconscious bias** is almost the opposite of the halo effect. The more a candidate is different from the interviewer, the more conscious effort is required to regard that person in a positive or even neutral light. This is a fundamental characteristic of

21

being human. Despite one's philosophical, ethical, or moral beliefs, human beings tend to form social groups with people who share similar attitudes, lifestyles, educational backgrounds, cultures, languages, etc. When a candidate appears to be different in some way, there is always an effect. This effect may be large, or it may be small. It may be good, or it may be bad. The important thing is to recognize the subjective nature of personal interviewing.

The "Great at Interviews" Candidate is dynamic, enthusiastic, quite personable, and remarkably well-informed about the company. This candidate is impeccably groomed and displays a polished, professional appearance. The toughest interview questions are answered with a refreshing combination of candor and confidence. Unfortunately, this outstanding skill at interviewing is not matched by job performance. The ability to talk knowledgeably about baseball and look good in a uniform does not necessarily translate into the ability to hit a 95 mph fastball.

> *" The ability to talk knowledgeably about baseball and look good in a uniform does not necessarily translate into the ability to hit a 95 mph fastball."*

The "Bad at Interviews" Candidate is quiet, uncomfortable, and nervous. Their appearance is lackluster and undistinguished. Interview questions are answered with hesitation or ambivalence. Information must be drawn out of the candidate, and few questions if any, are asked about the company. Sometimes however, such a candidate when hired, is discovered to be like a wonderful restaurant with no sign; the food is delicious, but not many people know to go there.

22

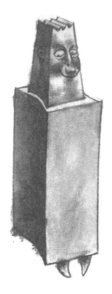

Timing can be everything. The interviewer flies into town on a late flight; stays at a bad hotel; has a sleepless night; and chokes down a cold breakfast with lousy coffee. The attitude and expectations awaiting the first candidate of the day are problematical at best. Prior to the afternoon session, the interviewer takes time for a relaxing and enjoyable lunch with old friends. Certainly the candidates fortunate enough to be scheduled after that interlude will meet with a considerably different reception.

Skills Match is the degree to which the candidate's educational background, technical skills, previous job experience, and particular expertise matches those required for the position. Reference checks, job histories, certifications, and demonstrations are the best means by which to evaluate this. Certain types of jobs involve skills that can be tested. **Objective testing is always preferable in view of both selection effectiveness and legal considerations**.

Skills Match by itself cannot predict job performance. The world of professional sports is filled with examples of players gifted with undeniable skills who have never achieved the potential success seemingly promised by those talents. There are several factors that must be considered in evaluating a candidate's Skills Match.

23

The first of these is **Trainability of the Skills or Knowledge.** Company Fit and Job Fit are extremely difficult to change, and very expensive to change in terms of time, energy, and money. When both of those are satisfactory however, it is possible to significantly enhance an employee's skills or knowledge of most jobs. **If either Company Fit or Job Fit is unsatisfactory, it is almost impossible to increase performance with training or coaching.**

> *"If either Company Fit or Job Fit is unsatisfactory, it is almost impossible to increase performance with training or coaching."*

There is a selection bias that might be called the **Pedigree Effect.** This refers to the tendency of interviewers to apply a disproportionate positive bias to a candidate who graduated from a particular school; who worked for a particular company; played a particular sport; or who has some particular background in common with previously successful candidates. While that background may certainly be a contributing factor to job success, it must be kept in perspective and not seen as a bonafide predictor.

There are many positions which demand **specific sets of knowledge or technical expertise.** Research has shown that selecting for those positions often places a tremendous bias on that expertise. While that can be justified in very esoteric professions, in most cases it must be balanced by a consideration of Job Fit and Company Fit.

On a broader scale, one of the most common hiring myths is that **"highly intelligent people can do anything".** An example of this is hiring only candi-

24

dates with certain degrees or educational achievements. Job Fit research has proven that people actually perform best when they are fully engaged by the challenges of the job. That means that unless "highly intelligent people" are provided with a steady source of intellectual challenges, they become not only poor performers, but can even become counterproductive.

Job Fit is the degree to which the candidate's cognitive abilities, interests, and personality dynamics fit those required by the position. Current research shows us that each one plays a critical role in job success and tenure. All three must be considered and evaluated if the degree of Job Fit is to be determined. These characteristics can only be accurately measured by using Job Fit assessment instruments.

Cognitive abilities refer to factors such as how quickly a person learns and what type of learning is most effective. In a business sense, this is a far more useful measurement than what is generally called intelligence. "Intelligence" is too often construed to mean how smart someone is, the implication being that there is a limited amount of knowledge that people can learn. Actually, given unlimited time, most people can potentially learn anything. The problem is that in the real world, and especially in the world of business, time is the limiting factor.

25

It is critical to match an employee's cognitive abilities with those required for the job. For example, people who are exceptionally fast problem solvers thrive in a challenging environment. When placed in relatively routine situations, those same people quickly become bored, resulting in unexpected turnover. People who learn more slowly become frustrated in environments that do not allow the time needed to assimilate key information about the job.

Interests refer to whether a person has a preference for working with people, data, or things. An individual may be capable of performing certain tasks, but may not be interested in those tasks. If that is the case, the person will probably not perform the tasks very well, nor for very long.

"Core personality is made up of traits that have been conditioned over many years. Such traits are critical in assessing a candidate's ability to perform virtually any aspect of any job."

The third part of Job Fit is the core personality of the candidate. This refers to the measurable characteristics of behavior that determine how the employee will behave in any situation. Core personality is made up of traits that have been conditioned over many years. Such traits are critical in assessing a candidate's ability to function as part of a team, ability to close a sale, ability to make decisions, ability to handle customers, and ability to perform virtually any aspect of any job.

Company Fit, Skills Match, and Job Fit are each an integral part of understanding job performance. Each is a necessary part of any hiring decision. Their relationship can best be understood by this example from the world of professional basketball. Imagine that an NBA team needed a starting center. The coach speaks to a candidate by phone who is enthusiastic about playing for that team and that

26

coach (Company Fit). The candidate has lightning speed, incredible ball-handling skills, and has never missed a free throw (Skills Match). The coach invites the player for a visit, and when the candidate walks onto the court, the coach sees that he is five feet tall (Job Fit)! Very quickly the player, his coach, and his teammates would realize that no matter how fast or how accurate his shotmaking, he would live in a world of armpits and elbows. No amount of coaching; no amount of extra training; and no amount of incentives could compensate for the lack of Job Fit.

Still seeking a starting center, the coach locates another candidate. This one is also enthusiastic about the team and the coach (Company Fit), but this one is seven feet tall (Job Fit)! The excitement vanishes however, when it is learned that despite his height, the candidate has never played basketball (Skills Match). There is just not enough time to bring his skills up to the level necessary for success in the NBA.

The frustrated coach then discovers a third candidate who plays like Michael Jordan (Skills Match) and who is seven feet tall (Job Fit). Unfortunately this player's attitude is so obnoxious that the rest of the team will quit if he starts (Company Fit).

Ideally the coach must find a player who matches in each part. **Superior skills can compensate for moderate Job Fit. Excellent Job Fit can compensate for moderate Company Fit. An infinite number of successful combinations are possible. It is the overall picture that is decisive... the picture of the Total Person.**

Chapter 3

THE ROLE OF TESTING & ASSESSMENTS IN THE SELECTION PROCESS

"If management can acquire better information on people, they will inevitably make better decisions."

28

THE ROLE OF TESTING & ASSESSMENTS IN THE SELECTION PROCESS

The principal reason to integrate testing and assessments into a selection process is to increase the level of information available for decision making. Today job applicants have an incredible range of resources to assist them in their job search. Professional resource writers stand ready to produce typeset, literary works of art, custom-designed to match specific jobs. Hundreds of books have been written to prepare applicants for any type of interview. Video taping of practice interviews with coaching advice is often used. All of this is largely directed at a population of interviewers who are experts in other areas of business, not interviewing; who have had little training; who have little time; and who do not interview often enough to build much experience.

Interviewing professionals using the most sophisticated techniques and with unlimited time, will select effective performers about 70% of the time. The inescapable problem is that human beings base much of their decisions on subjective and emotional responses. In fact, studies have shown that most hiring decisions are actually made within the first five minutes of the interview.

Testing and assessments are never a substitute for personal interviewing. The information provided by effective instruments can enable even average interviewers to produce results beyond any professionals' without

THE ROLE OF TESTING & ASSESSMENTS IN THE SELECTION PROCESS

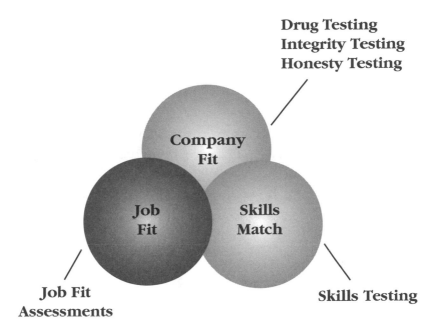

Drug Testing
Integrity Testing
Honesty Testing

Job Fit
Assessments

Skills Testing

The ideal candidate will fit in each part. The degree to which they do not fit is the gap in performance which you must fill with training, coaching, or changes in the job itself.

30

testing. This chapter is designed to explain the various types of testing and how each type plays a specific role in solving the problem of hiring top performers.

HONESTY & INTEGRITY TESTING

Honesty and integrity tests have been defined as written tests designed to identify individuals applying for work, who have relatively high propensities to steal money or property on the job, or who are likely to engage in behavior of a more generally counterproductive nature. Counter productivity may include such things as tardiness, absenteeism, sick leave abuse, and other forms of "time theft" (Office of Technology Assessment 1990).

Test publishers have gauged the effectiveness of their instruments by pointing to outcome criteria such as the reductions of employee theft or reductions in other counterproductive behaviors. Certainly businesses have strong incentives to consider such testing, not only as a cost control measure, but as a risk management issue considering the rise in negligent hiring litigation.

Honesty and integrity tests play an important role in determining Company Fit for many jobs, but unlike Job Fit assessments, there is not a clear differentiation of quality or effectiveness within the honesty and integrity testing industry. Conversely, the concepts of personality and intelligence have been researched

31

extensively throughout this century, and there is now a common foundation of knowledge. It is upon that common knowledge that current cognitive and personality instruments are based. Honesty and integrity tests however, have been created in response to employee theft problems. As many testing companies sought to answer the problems, there appeared an assortment of competitive solutions. Each is marketed by its respective publisher, and is often marketed in a confusing variety of forms.

The challenge of selecting the right instrument for a specific purpose is complicated by the diversity of approaches taken by the various test publishers. Essentially two elements must be examined: the constructs upon which the test is based and the research data that validates those constructs. Almost all research however, is conducted by the test publishers themselves, with very little data from independent sources.

> *"The challenge of selecting the right instrument for a specific purpose is complicated by the diversity of approaches taken by the various test publishers."*

There are several companies that have substantially demonstrated the effectiveness of their systems. They offer such a diverse assortment of applications however, that it is difficult to make a blanket recommendation, as there are significant legal and ethical considerations when implementing honesty and integrity testing. The legalities can also vary dramatically from state to state. Of course, any test must be in compliance with state and federal hiring guidelines and with the EEOC and the ADA. It is best to review the specific parameters of each situation before making a decision.

32

DRUG TESTING & SCREENING

In addition to the numerous chemical tests for substance-abuse, several companies incorporate a substance-abuse construct into their integrity tests. Some of these have proven to be successful as an initial screen prior to administration of a chemical test. It is generally observed that a positive score on a pencil-and-paper test will be followed by a positive score on a chemical test. Therefore a company can realize a cost per screen savings by administering the pen-and-pencil test first, and then exiting those who test positive.

As in the use of honesty and integrity testing, the universe of substance-abuse methodology is so diverse that each situation must be considered carefully and individually before a recommendation can be made. The legalities are particularly sensitive and complex.

There are a limited number of SAMHSA–NIDA (Substance Abuse and Mental Health Services Administration formally National Institute of Drug Abuse) certified laboratories in the United States, and each one provides chemical drug testing services. While ostensibly each of these laboratories offers a similar end product, there can be substantial differences in how that product is delivered.

A very important aspect of service is the turnaround time or the length of time before the test results are received by the client. Times at the various SAMHSA–NIDA labs range from 24 hours to over 72 hours for a normal negative result. Some positives may take much longer in some labs. This can be a critical difference in a competitive labor market, where any unnecessary delay can lose a good candidate to another employer.

> *"A very important aspect of service is the turnaround time or the length of time before the test results are received by the client."*

Another element of quality that is essential when selecting a source for drug testing is confidence in that laboratory's chain-of-custody procedure. The leading labs use a sophisticated bar coding system to insure specimen confidentiality and integrity by eliminating human error. This attention to detail can prove invaluable in the event of litigation.

If a company is using drug testing with a large volume of candidates and employees, another service feature that is beneficial is that of data management. This can be instrumental in implementing random selection policies and in maintaining efficient records.

Drug testing is an area of intensive research and innovation. Every day new products and services are coming into the marketplace in response to the growing problem of substance abuse. Some leading companies have developed on-site drug testing products, using the latest technologies. When properly used, these methodologies can provide forensic quality testing with negative results available in just minutes.

34

This can be a significant advantage when an immediate decision is desirable. Non-negatives still must always be confirmed in a laboratory. This type of testing can offer substantial economic savings also.

Drug testing is fast moving from being a preventive measure to becoming a marketing advantage in many industries, both in the eyes of consumers and in the eyes of potential employees. Eventually it will become standard in virtually all industries. Many laboratories provide a full range of training programs and materials. Assistance is even available to guide a company in developing a strategic plan to become Drug-Free.

"Drug testing is fast moving from being a preventive measure to becoming a marketing advantage in many industries, both in the eyes of consumers and in the eyes of potential employees."

The drug testing marketplace can be complex and confusing for non-professionals. There are many possible solutions for every situation, and in most cases, there is not one right answer. It is best to explore a variety of options, and as always, seek experienced advice.

SAFETY, RELIABILITY AND OTHER ASSESSMENTS

Various test publishers have developed constructs that measure such concepts as employee reliability, safety attitudes, call reluctance, customer service attitudes, tenure, attitudes toward supervision, responsibility, nonviolence, quality attitudes, and many others. While there is much that can be learned from some of these

35

products, they fall outside the main body of traditional assessment research. Each must be carefully considered with regard to its validity and the purpose for which it is used. In general, it is best to start an analysis with the basic Job Fit issues like cognitive abilities, interests, and personality, which have been established for quite some time. Once that foundation is understood, the more esoteric or specialized instruments can be helpful in fine-tuning individual performance.

SKILLS TESTING

Objective skills testing can be an important part of any hiring or placement decision. Certain categories of jobs, such as clerical positions, are more suitable for standardized testing than are many others. Computer-based skills testing is widely used to assess skill levels at using word processing programs, data bases, spread sheets, and other common software applications. Testing is also available for basic office functions, including filing, calculating postage, alphabetizing, etc. Many technical positions have devised tests on understanding specialized terminology or equipment. There are even dexterity tests for workers on small parts assembly lines, and mechanical understanding tests for maintenance positions.

As with all forms of testing, it is critical to insure the proper compliance with all state and federal guidelines, and to insure compliance with the EEOC and the ADA. The diverse nature of skills testing and the infinite job

possibilities make it essential to consider each situation individually before making any recommendations.

JOB FIT ASSESSMENTS

Three elements must be considered for a complete evaluation of Job Fit : Cognitive Abilities, Interests, and Personality.

Cognitive ability is the oldest job success indicator. Early measures of this were based on IQ tests or simple reasoning tests. Today more advanced assessments can measure specific abilities such as logical reasoning, problem solving, verbal reasoning, spatial reasoning, and conceptual thinking. When these abilities are more defined, they can better be applied to exact job requirements.

An individual's speed of learning is an important factor in the business world. Research has shown that the relationship between learning speed and job fit has a critical impact on issues such as turnover, safety, communications, training effectiveness, and many other areas of job performance. As discussed earlier, the myth exists that if "smart" people are hired, they will learn faster and perform better. The misunderstanding stems from the question of what exactly is "smart"? Matching learning speed with the demands of the job is a much more practical and effective concept for business decisions.

Those people who learn rapidly and solve problems quickly need a constant supply of new challenges and new problems with which to exercise their abilities. Lacking these, they can become bored or careless, often even creating their own set of challenges. Those people who learn a bit more slowly are fully engaged by routine jobs, finding in them a continual challenge, requiring their best efforts.

Interests are the second element in Job Fit.
The U.S. Department of Labor Dictionary of Occupational Titles codes job classifications with a rating of the complexity of the job functions in relation to working with People, Data, and Things. Interests have an important impact on tenure and performance. A person may have both the cognitive abilities and the personality to perform a particular job well. If the interests are not a good match however, the person will not want to do the job very long, and while there, will seldom bring their full attention to it.

"Those people who learn rapidly and solve problems quickly need a constant supply of new challenges and new problems with which to exercise their abilities."

The measurable dynamics of an individual's personality are the third element of Job Fit. This must be clearly differentiated from personality types, such as those found in early assessment instruments. Instruments based on personality types, such as DISC, the Enniagram, or Myers-Briggs, attempt to sort individual behavior into a number of various categories or types. By understanding the characteristics of each type, one can gain a limited insight into the mechanisms of human interaction. These simplified approaches serve as an

38

introduction to the concept of personality differences. The generalized nature of the information, while interesting and helpful, often lacks the precision needed for serious business decisions. The more advanced instruments provide quantified measurements of discrete elements of personality. This provides a clear picture of individual differences in performance and behavior. The list on the next page contains some of the job performance issues that are directly driven by personality.

39

Personality-Driven Job Performance Issues

Effective delegation

Maintaining discipline

Handling stress

Dealing with rejection

Closing sales

Team participation

Response to competition

Following rules

Innovative thinking

Attention to details

People skills

Time management

Brainstorming

Negotiating

Listening

Presentation skills

Sense of urgency

Quality management

> *" The core elements of personality are the foundation of all human behavior and interaction."*

There are an infinite number of possible listings. The core elements of personality are the foundation of all human behavior and interaction. The ability to accurately measure these core elements with modern assessment technology provides extraordinary information for management, which can be used in the selection process and after hiring (See Using Testing & Assessments with Existing Employees).

Chapter 4

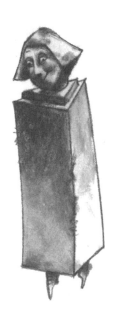

THE EVOLUTION OF ASSESSMENT TOOLS

"Fifth Generation information, when fully understood and internalized by management, will revolutionize the paradigm of how businesses manage performance and people."

THE EVOLUTION OF ASSESSMENT TOOLS

The idea of predicting job performance through the use of assessment instruments has long been a dream of the business world, but it has been an elusive dream. The extensive testing programs sponsored by the U.S. Army encouraged industries to try countless methods over the last fifty years to somehow predict the success of job candidates. For the most part, while some of these seemed promising, they never quite fulfilled the expectations. The idea had simply outrun the available technology and research. That reality, coupled with the changing tides of legal issues, served to dampen business' enthusiasm for assessments. Ironically, it is the legal environment, and the increasingly competitive marketplace that has awakened an intensified awareness of the power of assessment information.

There are over 500 assessments sold in the U.S. market alone. Many of them are based on older psychological theories and still use some of the original psychometric techniques. Early counseling instruments are often sold as hiring tools. The difficulty is that to the average business person, most assessment reports look similar. The instruments may look similar. The terminology used may even appear to be the same. Much as when buying a computer, the technical differences are blind to the user, and it is only the differences in performance that become apparent. Often the buyer must depend on a salesperson with limited knowledge of current technology. The following construct outlines the qualitative evolution of assessment instruments, as they progressed log-

43

ically from simple word lists to the leading psychometric tools available.

The diagram on the following page separates the population of assessment instruments into categories which reflect the qualitative evolution of the industry. This is by no means a comprehensive listing. There are hundreds of instruments and multiple variations of many of those. Most of those instruments are excellent choices for certain purposes. This is intended to provide a frame of reference by which businesses may select the appropriate tool for their needs.

The Evolution of Assessment Tools

	CHARACTERISTICS	EXAMPLES
FIFTH GENERATION	NORMATIVE COGNITIVE, INTERESTS, PERSONALITY QUANTIFIED SCALES (STEN) VALIDITY SCALES (4) MULTI-CULTURAL DESIGNED FOR BUSINESS USE	**THE PREVUE**
FOURTH GENERATION	NORMATIVE COGNITIVE AND PERSONALITY QUANTIFIED SCALES (STANINE) ADAPTED FOR BUSINESS USE	PROFILE USA PROFILE CANADA
THIRD GENERATION	NORMATIVE DIAGNOSTIC QUANTIFIED SCALES VALIDITY SCALES	MMPI (Clinical) 16PF (Clinical) CPI
SECOND GENERATION	PERSONALITY AND MORE COMBINATION OF METHODS NARRATIVE REPORTS	BIRKMAN CALIPER CHALLY
FIRST GENERATION	SIMPLE BEHAVIORAL STYLES/TYPES FAKEABLE PHRASES, TRUE-FALSE, ETC. NARRATIVE REPORT	MYERS-BRIGGS OMNIA WONDERLIC CPP ENNEAGRAM
	SIMPLE BEHAVIORAL STYLES FAKEABLE FORCED WORD CHOICES IPSATIVE SCORING NARRATIVE REPORT	DISC McQUAIG TIMMS PPA PERFORMAX CLEAVER
	SIMPLE BEHAVIORAL STYLES FAKEABLE SIMPLE WORD CHECKLIST NARRATIVE REPORT	PREDICTIVE INDEX AVA ITS PRO SCAN SURVEY

45

First Generation assessments are divided into three groups. The simplest of these are variations of an adjectival checklist developed over twenty-five years ago by David Merrill. The participant selects words which he feels are descriptive of his behavior as seen by others and as seen by himself. Such tests are extremely quick and inexpensive. It is quite easy however for the participant to select those words which portray the most favorable description.

Perhaps the largest group of First Generation assessments is that of the DISC-type instruments. The most common of these uses sets of four words or phrases in which the participant is required to select the one that most describes him and the one that least describes him. The resulting narrative report is based upon a theory of simple behavioral styles. These tools can be used to create interactive workshops that are fun and interesting, particularly to audiences which are unsophisticated with regard to psychometric testing. The danger is that often too many applications and too many conclusions can be based on a very small foundation of data. Forced choice questioning also generates ipsative scores which cannot be used to create meaningful norms used in analyzing Job Fit.

> *"The danger is that often too many applications and too many conclusions can be based on a very small foundation of data."*

The next group of First Generation instruments uses various methodologies and combinations of methods. These include answering true-false questions, selecting from a group of phrases instead of words, rating responses to certain situations, and a variety of other approaches.

There are three fundamental problems with all First Generation assessments:

1. Few actually measure personality traits. Instead, participants are sorted into simple behavioral styles or personality types. Cognitive ability, long-recognized as a critical element in Job Fit, is not addressed.

2. They are fakeable, consciously and subconsciously. On a conscious level, with many of these instruments, the participant has the ability to distort the results in a favorable direction without any indication of that in the report. On a subconscious level, **First Generation tools measure states, not traits.** States are subject to fluctuations of mood and emotion, and can vary significantly over relatively short periods of time. This dramatically reduces the test-retest reliability of First Generation instruments. Traits are part of our core behavior that seldom changes.

3. Most First Generation assessments rely heavily on narrative reports which are problematical for all generations. The meaning of words is intrinsic to people, not to the words themselves. For example, the adjective "outgoing" suggests vari-

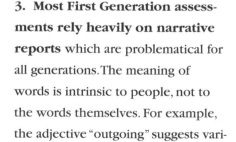

"The meaning of words is intrinsic to people, not to the words themselves."

47

ous pictures depending first on individual definition. More importantly, an extroverted reader sees a completely different picture than an introverted reader.

Second Generation assessments include a number of excellent instruments which measure various combinations of personality, behavioral styles, reasoning, interests, crystallized knowledge, numerical skills, or other attributes. Also included are systems that rely on batteries of assorted assessments to provide data for an overall report. While each of these methods offer some useful information, all fail to achieve the comprehensiveness, accuracy, reliability, specificity, or ease of use that is characterized by later Generations.

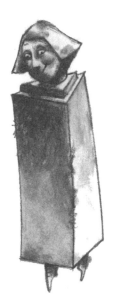

The principal problems involving Second Generation instruments are:

> **1. Most depend upon narrative reports with the same shortcomings described above.**

> **2. Many are vulnerable to faking or exaggeration, having questionable validity scales, if any.**

> **3. Some are dependent upon expert interpretation, either by a psychologist or a certified specialist.**

Third Generation assessments are remarkable psychometric instruments, providing accurate measurements of many of the complex characteristics of human behavior. With quantified scales and validity checks to prevent undetected faking, Third Generation assessments are important diagnostic tools for industrial psychologists, clinical psychologists, and psychiatrists, providing insight into the psychoses and neuroses of their patients.

It is this diagnostic nature of Third Generation Assessments that presents problems for business usage.

> *"It is this diagnostic nature of Third Generation Assessments that presents problems for business usage."*

1. **The Americans With Disabilities Act, the Civil Rights Acts, and other regulations expressly prohibit many of the questions found in these instruments. Soroka vs. Dayton Hudson Corp.** is an important case on hiring practices, in which Target Stores used Third Generation instruments as a part of their selection process.

2. **Third Generation assessments are dependent upon expert interpretation by psychologists or psychiatrists.** Consequently, the information is not readily understood by the average person.

49

Fourth Generation assessments combine measurements of cognitive ability with quantified scales of personality traits. They also contain validity scales to detect faking and equivocation. Fourth Generation tools have quantified scales, and their normative construction allows for the creation of job patterns. They are designed to be used by businesses, and can be understood by non-experts. In 1972, the main Fourth Generation instrument, the Profile Evaluation, became the first major normative instrument to use actual employees for its psychometric study. **While this certainly represented a milestone in its day, the passage of time has revealed several shortcomings.**

1. **Current psychometric theory acknowledges that studies must be revisited about every three years.** In the twenty-four years since the original Profile studies, the population has changed dramatically. Minorities little known in 1972, have grown to significant portions of the working population. **The social attitudes and values that are prevalent today are far from those of 1972. The effect of this disparity is that the scales contain significant inherent errors when measuring the population of the 1990's.**

> *"Current psychometric theory acknowledges that studies must be revisited about every three years."*

2. **Several scales in the mental abilities section measure crystallized knowledge (i.e. specific knowledge that is dependent on cultural environment and education)** rather than fluid knowledge (i.e. fundamental reasoning ability independent of specific content).

Fifth Generation assessments measure each of the three major areas of job fit: *cognitive abilities, interests, and personality.* They produce quantified scales that are easily used by non-experts, and they can be used to generate job patterns, analyzing the job fit reasons affecting the performance of individuals or teams. Fifth Generation instruments incorporate several validity scales to detect faking, exaggeration, or equivocation. The Prevue, which is currently the only Fifth Generation assessment available, has four validity scales. The Prevue is also the first major instrument to be designed specifically for use in business. **Fifth Generation instruments are developed in compliance with the legal requirements of the United States, Canada, and Great Britain, and actually serve to document non-discriminatory hiring practices when used consistently as recommended.**

> *"Fifth Generation instruments are developed in compliance with the legal requirements of the United States, Canada, and Great Britain."*

While Fifth Generation instruments offer significant advantages, several things must be considered:

1. Time and accuracy are the two inescapable trade-offs in psychometrics. Fifth Generation instruments require 50-70 minutes for completion. The generation of accurate and reliable data across the range of cognitive, interest, and personality scales demands a minimum number of items (questions) per scale. As

51

Fifth Generation instruments focus their reports on the core elements of cognitive, interests, and personality, it is difficult to see any scale as unnecessary, regardless of the job category.

2. Fifth Generation instruments offer remarkable accuracy and reliability which enable the information to be used in a number of applications that were not possible with older technologies. Realizing the full potential of these applications requires the commitment of training time for all key people managing the performance of people.

3. Fifth Generation information, when fully understood and internalized by management, will dramatically change the paradigm of how businesses manage performance and people.

The following page is a matrix of recommended applications for the Generations of assessments. It is important to understand that just as the most advanced computers are capable of more applications than early ones, so it is that Fifth Generation assessments are recommended for more applications than earlier ones. Recommendations are based upon many factors, including legal compliance, accuracy, reliability, validity, ease of use, comprehensiveness of information, etc. **It is important to know that all assessments are suitable for some uses. No assessment is suitable for all uses.**

> *"It is important to know that all assessments are suitable for some uses. No assessment is suitable for all uses."*

Recommended Applications
for the Generations of Assessments

APPLICATIONS	GENERATIONS				
	1st	2nd	3rd	4th	5th
Career Development	★	★	●		★
One-on-One Counseling	★	★	●		★
Pre-Employment Selection					★
Interviewing	★	★	●		★
Promotion Decisions			●		★
Simple Team Building	★	★			
Team Engineering					★
Sales Strategies		★			★
Performance Problems					★
Day-to-Day Management		★			★
Training Strategies		★	●		★
Re-Engineering					★
Rightsizing					★
Clinical Diagnosis			●		

★ RECOMMENDED　　　　● PROFESSIONALS ONLY

☐ OPTIONAL　　　　▨ NOT RECOMMENDED

54

Chapter 5

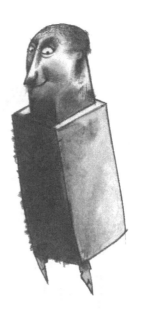

THE LEGALITIES OF USING TESTING & ASSESSMENTS

"The reality is that the proper and consistent use of effective testing and assessment systems can dramatically strengthen a company's legal position."

LEGALITIES OF USING TESTING & ASSESSMENTS

There are many misunderstandings regarding the legal use of testing and assessments in the business world. Certainly there is a maze of federal and state regulations and guidelines that can easily intimidate the average business person. The media has all too often publicized some rather dramatic misuses of testing, creating the impression that it is an all but certain recipe for disaster. It is reminiscent of a childhood memory of pleading for a BB gun for a birthday present, and being told that a BB gun would shoot out my eye, my friends' eyes, and even the eyes of total strangers. Both of these are fantastic exaggerations of a real, but manageable concern.

> *"The reality is that the proper and consistent use of effective testing and assessment systems can dramatically strengthen a company's legal position."*

The reality is that the proper and consistent use of effective testing and assessment systems can dramatically strengthen a company's legal position. Job-related testing and assessments are essentially the only way to document objective and non-discriminatory hiring practices. In the three-part paradigm of the selection process, illustrated by the three interlocking circles, the area most susceptible to bias or discrimination is Company Fit, which is largely determined by interviewing. Only the testing components are purely objective. Skills Match may or may not be measurable depending on the job. Only Job Fit, when measured by the proper assessment instrument, is completely objective. As Hogan (1990) correctly points out, **"Bias is a social com-**

57

ponent of the decision-making process, not a feature of the test result; therefore a primary advantage of test use is that tests, unlike interviewers, are incapable of being prejudiced by the applicant's race, gender, ethnicity, national origin, religion, age, or disability."

While this book is principally addressed to employers, it must be remembered that there are always two losers when an employee does not fit the job for which they were hired. The company loses the time, energy, and money spent on coaching and training, and of course, there is the loss of performance. Equally important is the employee's loss of the time and energy that is invested in the wrong opportunity. That part of their life cannot be replaced. The information provided by effective and properly used assessments can help each party arrive at the best decision. Every legal guideline and regulation supports that purpose. In fact, **it is inconsistent with the spirit of EEOC and ADA legislation to hire a person for whom the probability of reasonable success in the job is limited.**

> *"In fact, it is inconsistent with the spirit of EEOC and ADA legislation to hire a person for whom the probability of reasonable success in the job is limited."*

LEGAL CONCERNS

Consistent Application of Testing

There should be a standardized selection process for each position or job category. All applicants for the same position must take the same test or assessment at the same point in the process. It is not necessary to test everyone. It is not necessary to test everyone

within the same job category. *It is necessary to test everyone who reaches the same point in the process where tests or assessments are used.*

Job-Related Assessments

Tests and assessments are only valuable if they measure criteria that are directly related to job performance. This is necessary for legal compliance also. In the selection process, the greatest advantage in using assessments is using the information to predict the future performance of applicants. The ability to do this is not an intrinsic quality of any test. It is found in the relationship of the test results to the results of job performance, and this must be demonstrated through validation research.

> *"In the selection process, the greatest advantage in using assessments is using the information to predict the future performance of applicants."*

Adverse Impact

Under the Uniform Guidelines on Employee Selection Procedures (1994), a selection process must provide fair and equal employment opportunities to all applicants. **Testing may be used:**

1) to screen out those applicants who are not likely to be able to perform the job successfully

2) to group applicants in accordance with the likelihood of their successful performance

3) to rank applicants, selecting those with the highest scores for employment

The operative principle must always be to avoid any adverse impact or non-performance related discrimination against any minorities.

Quality of the Instrument
It is of critical importance that the instrument used in a selection process meet certain standards.

1) **The instrument should be copyrighted no earlier than 1991.** Two pieces of legislation that have directly impacted testing are the Civil Rights Act of 1991 and the Americans with Disabilities Act of 1990. The provisions of both of these acts must have been considered in the construction of any psychometric instrument used in making business decisions involving people.

"Many instruments which were originally validated for use in counseling and self-development are unfortunately marketed as hiring tools."

2) **The instrument must have been designed for use in a selection process.** Many instruments which were originally validated for use in counseling and self-development are unfortunately marketed as hiring tools. Validation is a major element of compliance, and validation is dependent upon two things. First, that the instrument has demonstrated that it measures what it claims to measure, and secondly, that it has demonstrated it under the same cir-

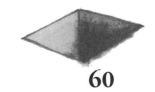

60

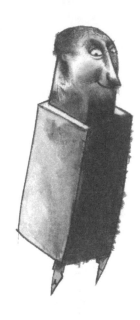

cumstances in which it is being used (ie. It is expected that an instrument used in the business environment would have used employed people in its psychometric studies).

3) The technical manual for the instrument must provide thorough documentation of

    a) the development of the scales used
    b) the development of the norms
    c) the various validation studies
    d) the diversity of the populations used in the studies
    (a robust sample would include several thousand people, representing a mixture of appropriate ages, sexes, cultures, and races).

4) The psychometric studies which generated the original norms should be revisited approximately every three years. This allows the instrument to adjust to changes in demographics and social values and attitudes.

Medical and Non-medical Tests

The **Americans with Disabilities Act ("ADA")** provides that no company shall discriminate against a qualified individual with a disability because of that disability in regard to hiring, advancement, training, or other elements of employment. **In a court of law, it can be assumed that if a company knew of a disability, that knowledge prejudiced their decisions.** The ADA therefore, in Section 12112(d), prohibits medical examinations or medical inquiries of a job applicant as to whether the applicant is an individual with a disability or as to the nature or severity of such disability. It is important to understand that this prohibition only refers to "medical examinations and inquiries". This refers to actual "*medical*" examinations regarding an applicant's "*medical condition or history*" which is designed to establish whether that individual is suffering from a *physical or mental illness.*

> *"In a court of law, it can be assumed that if a company knew of a disability, that knowledge prejudiced their decisions."*

The ADA goes on in Section 12112(d) to address acceptable inquiries, when it states that a company "may make pre-employment inquiries into the ability of an applicant to perform job-related functions". **This clearly permits the use of assessment instruments such as job fit assessments and honesty tests when used properly.**

The EEOC Enforcement Guidelines on Pre-Employment Inquiries Under the ADA (1994) outlines the following critical points:

1) the purpose of the test –
Instruments measuring fundamental characteristics of cognitive abilities, interests, personality, honesty and habits are providing information that is directly related to the successful performance of a job. Instruments which measure such things as psychoses, neuroses, physical or mental disabilities, or other pathological issues are prohibited in the pre-offer stage of a selection process. *Medically-oriented tests may be given after a job offer has been made.*

2) Medical or non-medical instruments – Psychometric assessment instruments designed for medical purposes are normed on populations of individuals with some type of medical disorder (eg. The Minnesota Multiphasic Personality Inventory was originally normed on a population of abnormal individuals who were under clinical care. Using those norms, the MMPI can measure such factors as paranoia, schizophrenia, and other psychopathology.). Non-medical assessment instruments are normed on a population of individu-

als that is consistent with the population and purpose for which the instrument is to be used (eg. The Prevue Assessment was normed on a broad based population of normal, working individuals. Psychopathology was not a criterion of the population. As a result, the Prevue can only measure traits, abilities, and attitudes which are related to job performance. It is blind to pschopathology.)

3) Content of items – While an instrument may not be designed as a medical test or assessment, it is important to insure that none of the items (questions) which comprise the instrument constitute a "medical inquiry" concerning the existence, nature, or severity of a disability (eg. At times I have been so depressed, I sought professional counseling.) if it is to be used at the pre-offer stage.

> *"Armed with knowledge and reasonable awareness, any business can take advantage of the power of assessment and testing information to strengthen its legal compliance."*

Legal concerns are a fact of every part of business life, but they are manageable concerns. **Armed with knowledge and reasonable awareness, any business can take advantage of the power of assessment and testing information, and at the same time, strengthen its legal compliance.**

This is a general outline of the major legal considerations. **Unusual situations should be reviewed on a case by case basis.**

Chapter 6

USING JOB FIT ASSESSMENTS WITH EXISTING EMPLOYEES

"Have you ever worked with someone whose performance was not what you expected? Today, Job Fit Assessments can tell you why that happened and if it can be changed."

66

USING JOB FIT ASSESSMENTS WITH EXISTING EMPLOYEES

> *"the accuracy of later generations of assessments has created extraordinary possibilities for analyzing and understanding the performance of existing employees."*

Traditionally the use of testing and assessments has been focused on the selection process. Certainly this is the most economically advantageous opportunity. However, the accuracy of later generations of assessments has created extraordinary possibilities for analyzing and understanding the performance of existing employees.

Solving Performance Problems

Almost every manager or supervisor knows who their best employees are. They also know who their worst employees are. What they generally do not know is why people hired by the same methods, doing the same job, and managed by the same person perform so differently. Today Fifth Generation technology can answer that question. Furthermore, it can determine if the problem can be fixed. In many cases it can even suggest how to fix it.

In the beginning of this book, the difference between solving systems problems and solving people problems was discussed. For centuries, businesses have relied on observation, opinion, and emotion to solve people problems. Systems solutions were based on objective data, quantified data, and a common frame of reference. Modern assessments can provide that same level of data about people.

67

The concept of the three cornerstones of job performance that was recommended for selecting new employees, is also essential to understanding the performance of existing employees.

THE CORNERSTONES OF JOB PERFORMANCE

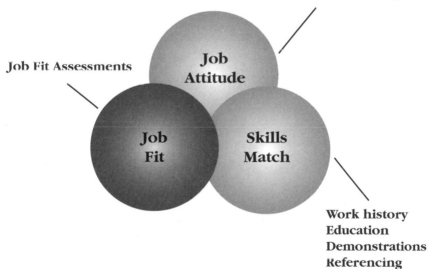

Interview Process
Validation Process
Drug Abuse Screening
Theft/Hostility Screening

Job Fit Assessments

Work history
Education
Demonstrations
Referencing

The Ideal Candidate Will Match In Each Part

In the case of current employees, Job Attitude is a more precise terminology than Company Fit. Successful workers typically have a "can do" attitude and believe in the value of the contribution of each employee. They are positive and enthusiastic and are happy with their work. Many factors affect this attitude, such as the company leadership, the environment, and of course, personal issues.

One of the classic responses to unsatisfactory performance has been the institution of a variety of motivational programs. These range from inspirational speeches and rallies to innovative incentive programs. New leadership strategies and visions are formulated and presented as the "new and improved" plan of the year. If Job Attitude is the only problem, motivational programs can work. If there is a more fundamental cause however, such programs can be expensive and frustrating.

> *"If Job Attitude is the only problem, motivational programs can work."*

The second part of the puzzle is Skills Match. An employee must have been trained for the job and provided with the necessary knowledge to accomplish the task. Unfortunately, it is common to find supervisors who have had no supervisory training; salespeople who have received only a suggestion of sales training; and production workers whose knowledge of safety procedures is only a haphazard collection of random comments.

Well-constructed training programs can have a tremendous positive effect on Skills Match. There are countless training resources available to every company, both internal and external. The difficulty arises when training is viewed as the Philosophers' Stone for performance without considering Job Fit.

Job Fit, as described earlier, is the degree to which the employee has the cognitive abilities, interests, and measurable personality traits which are necessary to perform the job successfully. When Job Fit is determined prior to training, the most effective training program is usually clear.

> *"When Job Fit is determined prior to training, the most effective training program is usually clear."*

For example, if a salesperson is making a large number of presentations but closes few sales, sending them to a all-purpose sales training program may not be the most effective course of action.

Example:

> **Salesperson A** is extremely extroverted, preferring to talk rather than listen. This makes for enthusiastic presentations, but because no questions are asked, no buying motives are established. The prospect is sold on the idea, but not on its application to him.

> **Solution A** might be for A to take a listening skills workshop and develop a question form for use with prospects.

> **Salesperson B** is bright and innovative, always thinking of new and better ways to sell the products. Unfortunately, this brilliant innovation generates an ever-evolving sales approach, sometimes better, sometimes worse. B is unable to build upon past successes or learn from failures because nothing is constant.

70

Solution B is to provide B with a skeleton sales path with at least a few milestones in concrete. It may be that if this product is sold successfully with a well-practiced script, B's fundamental personality is a poor match for this product. B would conceivably thrive with a more adaptable product or service which depended on a more consultative approach.

Salesperson C is extremely likable and has developed friendships with many of the prospects. C is knowledgeable about the product and delivers the sales presentation well. The problem is that C cannot stand confrontation of any kind, and closing a sale is unavoidably confrontational. After reading so many books on closing and listening to numerous tapes, C can usually ask for the order one or two times, yet when faced with the prospect's objections, C seizes the opportunity to withdraw until a more appropriate time.

"The critical point is that unless Job Fit is known, the best training anywhere is a hit-or-miss proposition. It can be frustrating for the employee and expensive for the business."

Solution C is not to increase C's collection of closing tapes and books. If this product's sale requires a series of strong closes, it would be best if C found another position, perhaps in the area of sales support. There C's ability to build relationships would flourish along with the sales.

There are countless variations and permutations to this scenario. The critical point is that unless Job Fit is known, the best training anywhere is a hit or miss proposition. It can be frustrating for the employee and expensive for the business. With Job Fit information, a multitude of effective options can be developed by any human resource professional, consultant, manager, or supervisor.

71

Team Engineering vs. Team Building

Personality assessments have been used for team building exercises since the first half of this century. As far back as ancient Greece, Hippocrates proposed that there were four basic types of personalities. He referred to them as Choleric, Sanguine, Phlegmatic and Melancholic. More recently, others have named their four types, Dominant, Influencing, Stable, and Compliant or Driver, Expressive, Amiable, and Analytical. Still other theories have identified eight types or nine types or some number of types. All of these typing methodologies are based upon behaviorism or behavioral style theory, a concept which is no longer supported in mainstream psychology.

Behaviorism postulated that the only source of data on personality was to be found in observed behavior. This led to the idea of behavioral styles, in which individuals were believed to have three sets of styles, their masks or what was required of them; their true styles or what was seen under stress; and the styles which they believed they had. Today psychologists recognize that individuals have a core personality which serves as the foundation of their behaviors under any situation. These core traits tend to remain relatively stable. This is good news since it would be difficult to function effectively if the internal compass points changed as often as behavioral styles suggested.

Team building exercises based upon these four quadrant instruments can be very productive however.

The concepts are simple and easily understood. The presentations can be remarkably entertaining. The construct is valid, and the instruments even appear to be rather accurate. The exercises usually do a superb job of describing each of the types and then explaining how each type relates or communicates with the other types. The problem is that there is no accurate way for those instruments to sort people into types. This is a very deceptive problem also. People tend to identify the areas in which the report seemed to be correct. It is far more difficult to identify the areas in which the report missed. Therefore participants in these kinds of seminars often adopt an unwarranted faith in the accuracy of these simple instruments. People become "typed". This is not unlike a "Four sizes fit all" theory.

> *"participants in seminars often adopt an unwarranted faith in the accuracy of simple instruments. People become typed."*

The most recent generations of assessment tools incorporate a total picture of cognitive abilities, interests, and personality. All of these factors play a key role in team interaction. More importantly, these newer instruments measure a range of discrete elements with considerable accuracy. This enables specific analysis of team fit. It also has the capability to deal with teams that are relatively homogenous or with work teams composed of specialized positions. The level of specificity possible is reflected in the designation of the process as team engineering.

73

Re-organization or Restructuring

The concept of Job Fit is integral to any plan for re-organizing a work force. Without it, the outcome of the process becomes largely a matter of luck or hope. Job Fit assessments can be used to statistically analyze both the old system and the new configuration. The existing population of employees can then be compared to the new requirements of Job Fit, and a strategic plan for the transition developed. Some employees will fit easily into the new design; others will be phased in with training; and the ones that cannot make the change can be identified.

Succession Planning

Succession planning is basically a matter of an internal selection process. Job Fit assessments allow the analysis of a executive's career path relative to the various Job Fits that are available. Even where experience demands a period of time in a position of marginal fit, that analysis enables a temporary adjustment of the expectations of performance during that period. This information can also be used to design individualized training curricula.

Summary

The new technology of performance information that is driven by the latest advances in testing and assessments will find its way into every aspect of management and business that involves people. This section has simply provided an overview of some of the more dramatic applications.

74

SUMMARY

Summary

I began this book by stating "Today, the use of assessment information is no longer an option. The legal environment demands it. Maintaining a competitive advantage requires it." To those business people who are thought leaders in their industries, these statements signal a window of opportunity. Competition has intensified in virtually every industry. The global economy has generated competitors that seem to defy geography. At the same time, the rapid advances in computers, telecommunications, and other technology, have enabled smaller companies to compete effectively with much larger corporations.

> *"Getting the right person in the right job quickly has become a decisive element in maintaining a competitive edge."*

The pace of change in the business world has accelerated beyond anyone's imagination. In this age of electronic information, a competitive edge based on a technological innovation is short-lived at best. Terms such as re-engineering, restructuring, right-sizing, and re-organization resound through the pages of every business periodical. The traditional recruiting definitions of "ambitious, hard-working, and loyal" have given way to "flexible, possessing a specialized set of abilities, and quick-to-learn". Business today can rarely tolerate indefinite learning curves. Getting the right person in the right job quickly has become a decisive element in maintaining a competitive edge. Success at this requires the information that only effective testing and assessments can provide.

77

The legal environment for businesses today has seldom been more treacherous. Newspapers report the flood of labor-related litigation and multi-million dollar settlements. Attorneys anxiously seek out opportunities for negligent hiring lawsuits. Special interest groups crusade against both real and imagined discrimination. Incidents of workplace violence and drug-related accidents underline the need for proper screening of potential employees.

In the last ten years, the laws and regulations affecting the selection of employees and the treatment of employees after hiring have become increasingly complex and restrictive. The paradox is that as employment decisions became more critical, the information that was traditionally available for those decisions has decreased. An example is the number of restrictions on the questions which can legally be asked in a pre-employment interview. Proper use of testing and assessments is virtually the only way to insure and to document objective and nondiscriminatory hiring practices.

> *"Proper use of testing and assessments is virtually the only way to insure and to document objective and nondiscriminatory hiring practices."*

It is often the case that within the seeds of adversity lies an even greater opportunity. Companies that use the latest assessment technology to strengthen their legal compliance will find it to be an incredibly powerful management tool. As this new level of information is integrated into executive thinking at all levels, businesses will discover that having the right person in the right job is the only lasting competitive advantage.

78

SOME RECOMMENDATIONS

"The financial impact of just one bad hire typically dwarfs the total amount spent on testing in the average size company."

SOME RECOMMENDATIONS

Once appropriate instruments have been chosen, the next important decision is where to apply them within the selection process. There is not one "right " or "correct" process that will serve well for all positions. Several factors can influence the construction of the most effective process for a particular job, but the fundamental rule of screening job applicants is to use the most accurate and least expensive method at the earliest point.

> *"a fundamental rule of screening job applicants is to use the most accurate and least expensive method at the earliest point"*

Accuracy is largely dependent on objectivity. Assuming that quality instruments are used and they are properly implemented, the following is a relative ranking in terms of objectivity and accuracy :

Most

1. Verification: criminal, driving, credit
2. Chemical drug testing
3. Skills testing
4. Job Fit assessments
5. Pencil & paper drug testing
6. Honesty & integrity testing
7. Referencing
8. Interviewing

Least

9. Resumés

This is by no means an exact listing. There are always variations in methods and in implementation, but the operating principle is to obtain the most objective information quickly. This enables the obvious decisions to be made as early as possible in the process (eg. If a

81

business is drug-free, there is little point in conducting extended interviews of a candidate who tests positive for substance abuse).

The next consideration is the cost of screening. This is not always easy to calculate. There are obvious factors such as the product cost of assessment instruments, but even greater costs are to be found in the time and energy of the managers, supervisors, human resource personnel, and employees who must administer any selection program. Testing and assessments can significantly leverage that time and energy by focusing their efforts only on those candidates who have passed earlier objective screens.

Time spent interviewing is the most common, undervalued expense in a selection process. Interviewing is a critical part of the job of managers and supervisors. It is productive however, to insure that any lengthy interviews be directed only at candidates who fit the job; who have had their work history referenced and verified; who are drug-free; who have the necessary skills and abilities; and who have met any other verifiable criteria. In-depth interviewing should be intended to identify the best candidate for the job from a field of pre-qualified applicants.

The cost of the testing and assessment instruments is variable depending on the product and the services offered. An often asked question is how much does a good instrument cost. This is much like asking how much to pay for a parachute. The answer

> *"Time spent interviewing is the most common, undervalued expense in a selection process."*

> *"An often asked question is how much does a good instrument cost. This is much like asking how much to pay for a parachute."*

82

is as much as it costs to be sure it will open. The parallel business answer might be as much as it takes to get the right person for the job and stay out of court. The best answer depends on the particulars of that situation. Ironically, the cost of testing and assessments is generally the least expense associated with a sound selection system. **The financial impact of just one bad hire typically dwarfs the total amount spent annually on testing in the average size company.**

> *"Ironically, the cost of testing and assessments is generally the least expense associated with a sound selection system."*

Recognizing that each situation must be considered individually to design the most effective system, the following diagram illustrates in general, where the various screening methods would be used. Specific situations may require rearranging certain screens, adding additional screens, or omitting some screens. Many variables must be considered, such as :

- the number of candidates available
- the number of applicants
- the set of skills and knowledge necessary for the job
- the number of selection personnel available
- the experience level of those personnel
- the number of locations involved
- the legal exposures involved
- the job's safety considerations
- the time available
- and others.

83

There are always trade-offs with any combination. In today's legal environment, it is better to over-screen than to take unnecessary and easily avoided risks.

The following are a series of examples in which various selection systems can be made more effective and/or economical.

Paper & Pencil Drug Tests and Chemical Drug Tests

A chemical drug test costs $30 per person, and a paper & pencil drug test costs $12 per person. By using the paper & pencil test first in the screening process, every applicant that tests positive at that point and is exited represents a savings of $18 because the chemical test is now unnecessary.

Job Fit Assessments and Interviewing Time

A job fit assessment costs $75 per person, and the sales manager's time is worth $200 per hour (IMPORTANT: THE COST OF THE INTERVIEWERS' TIME IS NOT THE HOURLY SALARY. IT IS THAT PLUS THE PRODUCTIVITY COST AND THE OPPORTUNITY COST OF THE TIME). By using job fit assessments to screen out the three top candidates from the pool of ten applicants, the cost is reduced to $750 from

84

$1000(assuming average interviews of only thirty minutes). In addition, the interviewer now has specific information on each of the candidates with which to guide the interviews.

Verification, Drug Testing, and Job Fit Assessments

A company wants to hire several truck drivers. Job fit assessments cost $75 each; verification of criminal records and driving records costs $60 each; and paper & pencil drug testing costs $12 each. Since any candidate who a) uses drugs; b) has a bad driving record; or c) does not fit the job would be unacceptable, each of these screens is important. The most economical arrangement is to apply the drug test ($12) first. Candidates testing positive will not require either of the other two screens. The next step is to verify criminal records and driving records ($60) for those candidates testing negative on the drug test. Anyone screened out at this point will not require the job fit assessment ($75).

Multiple Interviews and Job Fit Assessments

After initial interviews by the sales manager, a company traditionally has several of its top salespeople also interview the candidates. The group then meets to discuss their opinions. Finalists are then given job fit assessments. From an economic point of view, this is an extremely expensive process. Sales time and sales management time is a very limited and very valuable resource in every company. Spending that time on candidates that may not fit the job is an unnecessary expense. By assessing job fit prior to those interviews, costs are dramatically reduced, and with the job fit information in hand, the interviews will be significantly more productive.

Testing Only the Final Candidate for Job Fit

This is truly one of the tragic false economies that can occur in a selection process. When only the final candidate is tested for job fit, it is like trying to recruit a championship swimming team by asking the question, "Can you swim?". The only possible answers are "Yes" or "No". When five candidates are tested for job fit, the question becomes, "Who is the best swimmer?".

> *"When only the final candidate is tested for job fit, it is like trying to recruit a championship swimming team by asking the question, "Can you swim?". The only possible answers are "Yes" or "No".*

On-site Drug Testing and Turnaround Times

A company is in a highly competitive labor market, and routinely administers chemical drug tests to all qualified applicants. The samples are collected at the nearby hospital and sent to a major national laboratory. The cost is $35 per test and the typical turnaround time is 48-72 hours. While the company can make a conditional job offer, it finds itself at a disadvantage when competing for workers who receive

86

unconditional offers on the same day from other employers.

By switching to on-site testing, which is also conducted at a nearby medical facility, the company can determine negative results same day. This enables the company to make same-day offers without compromising its drug policy. Non-negative results are chemically confirmed in 24 hours.

An economic benefit of this process is that on-site testing costs $10 - $20 per test. This results in a savings of $15 or more for each negative result.

Testing and assessments play two important roles in selection. The first is to screen out potential problems :

- Substance abuse
- Slow learning curve
- History of theft
- Inability to work on a team
- History of tardiness
- Inability to deal with stress
- Safety problems
- Inability to handle conflict
- Hostility
- Inability to follow rules
- Turnover problems
- Inability to close sales
- Difficulty with change
- Communication problems
- and many others.

87

The second is to point out potential abilities and strengths that are needed for success :

- Fast learning curve
- Ability to work alone
- Consistent worker
- Strong closer
- Excellent people skills
- Good diplomat
- Flexible and adaptable
- Good conceptual thinking
- Creative problem solver
- Strong team member
- Ability to follow rules
- Quick decision-maker
- Effective delegator
- Stable employee
- and many others.

When both of these roles are recognized and understood, the true potential of advanced selection systems can be applied to any business.

QUESTIONS & ANSWERS

Questions & Answers

Q: **We use an industrial psychologist. Why should we consider assessments?**

A: Industrial psychologists play an important role by supplying a professional psychological opinion as a supplement to many decision-making processes. Several facts must be understood about that role.

a) The use of an industrial psychologist to supply information used for a hiring or placement decision in no way limits the exposure of the client company to federal and state regulations (e.g. If that information can be shown to be discriminatory, the decision can be shown to be discriminatory).

b) The psychologist's summary information is only as good as the assessments used to obtain the initial data (i.e. A psychologist using 1st or 2nd Generation tools cannot produce a 5th Generation quality of information).

Q: **We were considering creating our own tests. Wouldn't that be better?**

A: It depends completely on what you wish to measure. If there is some unique skill, ability, or knowledge that is critical to successful performance of a particular job, and there is not an existing instrument that measures that, it may be necessary to construct one. If however, success is dependent upon a

91

unique combination of fundamental characteristics of behavior and abilities, it is much
better to use established tools. The major
assessment instruments, like those of the
3rd, 4th, and 5th Generations, required years
to develop; thousands of people to partici-
pate in the normative studies; hundreds of
thousands of dollars; and the expertise
found in a relatively small number of psychometric experts. It is usually more economical and more effective to buy specialized expertise.

Q: **We use a customized interview system
that is very effective. Do we also need
testing?**

A: Customized interview systems, targeted
interviewing, and behavioral interviewing
are all very effective methods of identifying
potentially successful job candidates. Several
systems use what is called a biodata survey
to profile successful candidates and then
match interviewees to that profile. These
may use simple personality assessments as a
part of that process. Such systems can be
one of the most effective ways to identify
Company Fit, and in some cases even Skills
and Abilities. A complete picture of a candidate would still require a measure of Job Fit,
and a separate assessment instrument would
be necessary and desirable for that.

92

Q: **Our selection process is too long now. We don't have time to do testing too. Are there shorter tests?**

A: Unfortunately, asking for shorter assessments is much like asking the doctor for a cheaper prescription. There are cheaper ones, but they won't make you well. There are shorter assessments, but they don't measure much, and they don't measure it accurately. The inescapable trade-off in psychometrics is that it requires a certain number of items or questions to accurately measure each characteristic. Tests can only be shortened by limiting the scope of the instrument, or by sacrificing the accuracy of the results. A reasonable length of time for an effective business-oriented instrument is from 50 to 70 minutes.

Q: **I've heard that testing is not legal. Is that true?**

A: This is clearly not true. In fact, proper use of assessments can provide the most effective documentation of objective and nondiscriminatory hiring practices. The legality of any assessment instrument depends upon a combination of factors, including consistency of application, the validated purpose of the instrument, the job-related constructs of the instrument, and the incorporation of the results into the decision-making process. (For details, see previous section.)

93

Q : **We have used a First Generation instrument for years and everyone really likes it. Why should we change?**

A: First of all, you must separate the emotional feelings of familiarity from the pragmatic issues of effectiveness. People were once comfortable using typewriters and adding machines instead of computers. Today those same people complain about the "slowness" of their five-year old machines and dream about ultra-fast notebooks with color monitors and fax modems. The best slide rules do not even beg a comparison with the cheapest calculators, and the best instruments of the First Generation do not beg a comparison with those of the Fifth Generation.

People really want tools that work effectively and that make their jobs easier. The transition from First to Fifth is easily accomplished with training and strong management support.

Q: **Won't some people be offended by being asked to complete these tests?**

A: Certainly, but if some people are offended by a company's sincere and professional efforts to insure their success through effective job matching, it is a small price to pay for the overall benefits to all employees in the company.

Q: **Aren't there some people who just don't do well on tests?**

A: The inherent concept in assessment technology is that all people are good at something, but no one is good at everything. That includes testing. In general, most people are anxious about taking any kind of assessment. This reaction has been conditioned by years in school, where passing or failing tests determined the class standing. Other tests such as driving tests and medical tests also contributed to this attitude. This is why it is important to explain to all candidates what is the purpose of each test or assessment before it is given. Many of the latest instruments incorporate audio tapes or preliminary written messages designed to put the candidate at ease.

It is also important to recognize that people with poor skills will seldom be positively excited about taking a skills test. People with performance problems are seldom excited about taking a job fit assessment. That is precisely why tests are a vital part of the business world. Effective assessments can identify the critical areas that people do not want to reveal, but that the business must know to make the best decision.

95

Q: **We use recruiters for our key positions. Finding good people is their job. Why should we use testing?**

A: Professional recruiters can offer significant advantages in seeking candidates for any positions but these caveats are important in selecting the most effective recruiter for your needs:

1. Recruiters that are part of a national and even international network have a much greater range of resources. They can generally produce a variety of candidates in a shorter period of time.

2. The leading recruiters use Job Fit assessments to ensure that their candidates not only interview well and have the requisite skills and experience, but that they also match the Job Fit requirements of the client.

GLOSSARY

GLOSSARY

Affective - This refers to the non-intellectual aspects of behavior.

Aptitude - This traditionally refers to a relatively homogenous and clearly defined segment of ability.

Behavioral Styles - These refer to any of several categorizations of personality into a construct or matrix of characteristic types. These types are essentially models by which observed behavior and interaction may be discussed and understood. (Also called Social Styles)

Benchmark Pattern - This refers to a composite picture of the characteristics of top performers produced by assessing and analyzing a sample group. (Also called a Success Pattern or Success Profile)

Cognitive Abilities - These include various elements of intelligence, characterized as Reasoning, Numerical Reasoning, Verbal Reasoning, Spatial Reasoning, Mental Alertness, etc.

Construct - A psychological characteristic that is considered to vary across individuals. A construct is not directly observable, but it is a theoretical concept derived from research and experience that has been constructed to explain observable behavior patterns.

Core Personality - This refers to an individual's fundamental traits of personality that are established during childhood, and tend to remain the same over time in the absence of some life trauma.

Conative - This refers to the individual differences in motivational content or to the differences in the things for which people strive (Miller, 1991).

99

Equivocation - This refers to the set of responses that tend to choose the middle response of several extremes or the response that is the least committal. This has the effect of diluting the information provided.

Factor Analysis - Any of several methods of analyzing the intercorrelations or covariances among variables by constructing hypothetical factors, which are fewer in number than the original variables. It indicates how much of the variation in each original measure can be accounted for by each of the hypothetical factors.

Faking - This refers to attempts by the test participant to misrepresent their true behavior through exaggeration, distortion, equivocation, avoidance, or some other means.

Intelligence

Crystallized Intelligence - This refers to intelligence that is dependent upon culture, education, or experience.

Fluid Intelligence - This refers to raw intelligence or reasoning ability that is not dependent upon culture, education, or experience. Measurements of fluid intelligence are much more effective in predicting performance in diverse situations. Measures of fluid intelligence are less likely to create adverse impact problems.

Item - This refers to a question or a problem on an instrument.

Ipsative - This is a type of scoring generated by forced choice items (e.g. Select the word that MOST describes you and the word that LEAST describes you from the following: moody, thoughtful, enthusiastic, or intense.) It also refers to any type of scoring that compares the relative value of several dimensions within an individual. Norms developed using such instruments are "innocent of any psychological meaning." (Kline, 1993) These are much different than normative instruments which quantifiably measure dimensions using a normal scale. Normative data can be used effectively to benchmark "norms" for various jobs.

Item Analysis - The process of assessing certain characteristics of test items, usually the difficulty value, the discriminating power, and sometimes, the correlation with an external criterion.

Normative - This is a type of scoring produced by testing a large population and generating a normal bell curve distribution of the results. The distribution is then divided into standard tenths (or ninths in older instruments), creating a quantified, normal scale with which to measure and compare individuals.

Personality Types - These are categories of people who exhibit particular combinations of psychological characteristics, the assumption being that this combination is unique and distinguishes this type from another (Miller, 1991).

Psychometrics - The science of measuring the characteristics of human behavior, personality, cognitive abilities, interests, or aptitudes.

Reliability

Test-Retest Reliability - This refers to a test's stability over time. Lower test-retest reliability indicates that the instrument is not measuring core behavior traits, but is assessing states, which are subject to change with mood or circumstances.

Internal Reliability - This refers to the ability of a test to measure discrete variables. The degree to which variable measurement is cross-related lowers internal reliability.

Social Desirability - This refers to the set of responses in which participants tend to answer in such a way as to portray themselves in the most favorable light.

Social Styles - These refer to any of several categorizations of personality into a construct or matrix of characteristic types. These types are essentially models by which observed behavior and interaction may be discussed and understood. (Also called Behavioral Styles)

Standard Deviation - This is a measure of the variability of a sample of scores from the average or mean of that same sample.

Success Pattern or Success Profile - This refers to a composite picture of the characteristics of top performers produced by assessing and analyzing a sample group. (Also called a Benchmark Pattern)

Technical Manual - This is a step-by-step description of how the instrument was constructed. It outlines the various constructs used by the assessment, and the basis of their formulation. The numerous validity studies are detailed with the description of the various populations used in the studies.

102

Types - This refers to the concept of sorting people into various categories or sets of behavior for the purpose of discussing interaction. Early assessments were based on this concept.

Validity - A test is said to be valid if it measures what it claims to measure. There is no one validity coefficient for a test. A test is always valid for some purpose, and therefore is more valid in some circumstances than in others (Kline, 1993).
Deductive Validation starts with a theory in order that the content of the test is defined and that hypotheses are generated concerning what should correlate with the test scores.
Inductive Validation starts with the test measure and then tries to infer what it must be a measure of by examining its relationship with other things.

   Construct Validity - This refers to whether a test is measuring what it claims to measure as judged by accumulated evidence.

   Concurrent Validity - A test is said to have concurrent validity if it correlates highly with a "benchmark" test of the same variables.

   Content Validity - This refers to tests such as ability or attainment tests where the domain of items is very defined.

   Criterion Validity - This refers to evidence that shows the extent to which scores on a test are related to a criterion measure.

   Concurrent Criterion-Related Validity - This refers to evidence of criterion validity in which predictor and criterion information are obtained at approximately the same time.

103

Predictive Criterion-Related Validity - This refers to evidence of criterion validity in which criterion scores are observed at a later date (e.g. after job performance).

Face Validity - An instrument is said to be face valid if it appears to be measuring what it claims to measure.

Predictive Validity - A test is said to have predictive validity if it will predict some variable.

Synthetic Validity - This refers to the practice of using validity generalization to "synthesize" the criteria for a new job through extrapolation from known predictive criteria in other jobs.

Validity Generalization - This refers to applying validity evidence obtained in one or more situations to other similar situations on the basis of simultaneous estimation, meta-analysis, or synthetic validation arguments.

Validity Scales - This refers to any of a variety of scales designed to indicate exaggeration, faking, equivocation, or deception by test participants.

REFERENCES

References

Aiken, Lewis (1988). **Psychological Testing and Assessment**.

American Psychological Association (1985). **Standards for Educational and Psychological Testing**. Washington, DC.

Anastasi, Anne (1988). **Psychological Testing**, 6th ed. New York, MacMillan.

Baron, S. Anthony (1993). **Violence in the Workplace**. California, Pathfinder Publishing of California.

Bartram, David (1990). **Measuring Differences between People**. England, NFER-NELSON.

Bartram, David (1990). **Reliability and Validity**. England, NFER-NELSON.

Beech, John R. and Harding, Leonora (1990). **Testing People, A Practical Guide to Psychometrics**. England, NFER-NELSON.

Bell, Arthur H. (1989). **The Complete Manager's Guide to Interviewing - How to Hire the Best**. Illinois, Dow Jones-Irwin.

Bequal, August (1990). **Every Manager's Legal Guide to Hiring**. Illinois, Dow Jones-Irwin.

Bureau of National Affairs, Inc. (1990). **Uniform Guidelines on Employment Selection Procedures**.

107

Buros Institute (1990-1993). **The Mental Measurements Yearbooks**. University of Nebraska.

Clifton, Donald O. and Nelson, Paula (1992). **Soar With Your Strengths**. New York, Delacorte Press.

Coates, Dennis E. (1991). **A Comparison of Personality Assessments**. Virginia.

Congress of the United States, Office of Technology Assessment (1990). **Use of Integrity Tests for Pre-Employment Screening**. Washington, DC, U.S. Government Printing Office.

Cronbach, L.J. (1984). **Essentials of Psychological Testing**, 4th ed.

DuBois, P.H. (1970). **A History of Psychological Testing**.

Duston, Robert L. (1992). **The Effect of the ADA on Employee Selection Procedures**. University Publications of America.

EEOC and US Department of Justice (1991). **Americans with Disabilities Act Handbook**. Washington, DC.

French, Chris (1990). **Computer-Assisted Assessment**. England, NFER-NELSON.

Gardner, Howard (1992). **Frames of Mind**. New York, Doubleday.

Gardner, Howard (1993). **Multiple Intelligences**. New York, BasicBooks.

Gould, Steven Jay (1981). **The Mismeasure of Man**.

Gowing, Marilyn and Young, Ellen (1990). **Legal, Regulatory, and Professional Considerations in Personnel Testing**. Texas, PRO-ED.

Greenberg, Herbert and Greenberg, Jeane (1980). **Job Matching for Better Sales Performance**. Massachusetts, Harvard Business Review.

Hogan, Joyce (1990). **Employment Tests: History and User Considerations**. Texas, PRO-ED.

Hogan, Joyce (1990). **Business and Industry Testing**. Texas, PRO-ED.

Hogan, Robert (1990). **What Kind of Tests Are Useful in Organizations?**. Texas, PRO-ED.

Hopkins, Kevin R. and Nestleroth, Susan L. and Bolick, Clint (1991). **Help Wanted**. New York, McGraw-Hill, Inc.

Hunt, Morton (1993). **The Story of Psychology**. New York, Doubleday.

Jones, James E., Jr. (1987). **Cases and Materials on Discrimination in Employment, 5th ed**. St. Paul, West Publishing Co.

Jones, John W. (1990). **Megatrends in Integrity Testing**. Security Management.

Keyser, D.J. and Sweetland, R.C. (1984-1988). **Test Critiques (Vols. I-VII)**. Texas, PRO-ED.

Kline, Paul (1990). **How Tests Are Constructed**. England, NFER-NELSON.

Kline, Paul (1990). **Selecting the Best Test**. England, NFER-NELSON.

Kline, Paul (1993). **The Handbook of Psychological Testing**. London, Routledge.

Lee, Chris (1988). **Testing Makes a Comeback**. Training.

Malloy, John T. (1981). **Malloy's Live For Success**. Toronto, Bantam Books.

Martin, Justin (1990). **Workplace Testing - Why Can't We Get It Right?**. Across The Board.

Martin, Scott and Slora, Karen (1991). **Employee Selection by Testing**. HR Magazine.

Maurice, Samuel (1990). **Matching People and Jobs**. Executive Excellence.

Miller, Alan (1991). **Personality Types, A Modern Synthesis**. Canada, University of Calgary Press.

O'Connor, Michael and Mervin, Sandra (1988). **The Mysteries of Motivation**. Carlson Learning Company.

O'Meara, Daniel P. (1994). **Personality Tests Raise Questions of Legality and Effectiveness**. HR Magazine.

Paitiel, Laurence (1986). **Self-Appraisal Inventories**. The British Psychological Society.

Parry, Scott (1993). **How to Validate an Assessment Tool**. Training.

110

Riso, Don Richard (1992). **Discovering Your Personality Type**. Boston, Haughton Mifflin.

Schmidt, Frank and Ones, Deniz and Viswesvaran, Chockalingam (1994). **Psychologists Validate the Use of Integrity Tests**. MPPL.

Seligman, Daniel (1992). **A Question of Intelligence: The IQ Debate in America**.

Shelley, Douglas and Cohen, David (1986). **Testing Psychological Tests**.

Sparks, C. Paul (1990). **How to Read a Test Manual**. Texas, PRO-ED.

Sweetland, R.C. and Keyser, D.J. (1986). **Tests: A Comprehensive Reference for Assessments in Psychology, Education, and Business**. Texas, PRO-ED.

Tieger, Paul D. and Barron-Tieger, Barbara (1992). **Do What You Are**. Boston, Little, Brown, and Company.

Weiner, Elliot and Stewart, Barbara (1985). **Assessing Individuals - Psychological and Educational Tests and Measurements**. Boston, Little, Brown and Company.

Zemke, Ron (1992). **Second Thoughts About the MBTI**.

ABOUT THE AUTHOR

About the Author

Chuck Russell is the founder and managing partner of Moreland Russell, Inc., a unique consulting firm specializing in advising companies on how to integrate assessment technologies into their businesses. His pragmatic, common sense approach to solutions is a welcome relief from the theories and philosophies abounding among consultants.

This focus on practicality has been acquired first hand. Chuck has held senior management positions in two corporations. He has also bootstrapped the startup of three entrepreneurial companies of his own, two of which have been sold. During his sales career, Chuck ranked #4 and #10 out of over 2000 salespeople across the country. Moving into sales management, he directed that firm to top honors out of 700 other franchises for two consecutive years. In 1990, he founded The Russell Group, specializing in helping successful entrepreneurial companies deal with the challenges of rapid growth. That company was sold in 1995, and the assessment consulting business was concentrated into the current Moreland Russell with Chuck's five year business partner, Julie Moreland, a remarkably talented executive and consultant.

Moreland Russell has pioneered the use of the latest generations of assessment technology to create a new paradigm for understanding people and their performance. These concepts are revolutionizing virtually every decision-making process in business, from the selection of new employees to succession planning, and from team engineering projects to the day-to-day management of individuals. Properly implemented, the leading assessments offer a sustainable competitive advantage to innovative companies. Moreland Russell offers services ranging from objective recommendations on how to select the most

113

effective instruments to turnkey installations of systems. Moreland Russell's combined knowledge of psychometrics, psychology, testing legalities, and the assessment marketplace, is backed by 14 years of management consulting with successful companies of all sizes. The recommendations which are made are drawn from the general population of resources and are not limited to certain vendors or products. This objectivity has allowed Moreland Russell to avoid the magic wand approach of so many test salespeople.

Chuck is the creator of many innovations in the assessment industry, and he is the writer-director of several revolutionary video programs relating assessment information to day-to-day management practices. As a top-rated national speaker, he has been described as part visionary, part Southern evangelist, and part humorist, as he has introduced hundreds of audiences to a new understanding of people and performance.

Chuck is from Rome, Georgia and graduated from Spring Hill College with a degree in Economics. He is a former tennis professional and also owns golf clubs. He is married to an absolutely wonderful woman, Lauretta, and they have a four and one-half year old daughter, Lacey, and a two and one-half year old son, Jamey.

For information on booking Chuck Russell as a speaker or if you wish to discuss a project, please call Moreland Russell at (800) 849-7738.

For sdditional copies of this book contact publisher:
Johnson & James
12460 Crabapple Road
Suite 202-113
Alpharetta, GA 30201

114